KEEPING THE FAMILY TOGETHER

Amish Romance

HANNAH MILLER

Tica House
Publishing

Sweet Romance that Delights and Enchants!

Personal Word from the Author

To My Dear Readers,

How exciting that you have chosen one of my books to read. Thank you! I am proud to now be part of the team of writers at Tica House Publishing who work joyfully to bring you stories of hope, faith, courage, and love.

Please feel free to contact me as I love to hear from my readers. I would like to personally invite you to sign up for updates and to become part of our **Exclusive Reader Club** —it's completely Free to join! Hope to see you there!

With love,

Hannah Miller

VISIT HERE to Join our Reader's Club and to Receive Tica House Updates:

https://amish.subscribemenow.com/

Contents

Chapter One

Dear Journal,

Torrents came from the sky today. So many crops were destroyed—they just lay over and drowned. John, Mark, Stuart and I tried to save what we could, but it was a huge task. Even if our parents had still been alive to help us, I doubt if having their extra hands would have made any difference. Daed *would have conceded that it was a lost cause. I wish he and* Mamm *were still here, but I know that no amount of wishing or praying is going to bring them back.* Gott *called them home, and that is that...*

Karen laid down her pen. What more could she write? Sometimes a person just reached the end of the road. Sometimes there was nowhere to go.

Her black *kapp* strings hung loosely down in front of her onto the desk—the very desk her *daed* had made for her before... before he died of a heart attack. *Mamm* did not have to join him; she could have fought to stay alive for her *kinner*. Karen reached into her apron pocket and took out her handkerchief. She blew her nose and sat up straighter in her chair. *Was it noble to die of a broken heart over the loss of your man?*

For *Mamm* had died of a broken heart; of that, Karen was certain. Most folks would say it was impossible. They'd say she was being fanciful to even think such a thing. But in her own heart, she was certain. And now, she had been left alone to care for her three brothers, and she knew she was not doing a good job of it.

Her cheeks were flushed from the overcast sun she had toiled under all day. She put her hands flat on the desk and stared at them. She was only twenty-three, but stretched out in front of her, she saw the calloused hands of a fifty-year-old. She whispered to herself, *"Cast your burden on the Lord, and he will sustain you; he will never permit the righteous to be moved."*

The banging on her bedroom door pulled her from her well of sadness. "What is it? Must you bang?"

"Karen, there is someone here to see you. It is important."

She moaned. Everything was important to her ten-year-old brother. "Stuart, this had better be important. I am exhausted and—"

"It is, truly it is. Come out, Karen, please."

The urgency in his voice was a skill Stuart had mastered. She opened her bedroom door slowly, expecting him to fall into her room clutching a bleeding finger, or bearing a basket with a wounded creature.

"There is a man here. He says he is from a bank. John and Mark are still out in the field. So I had to come get you."

She opened the door all the way. "The bank? What did he say his name is?"

Stuart was small and frail for his age. He had been only seven when his parents passed. "He said his name is Jace London."

Karen knew the name. He was from the bank where the family had gotten two loans for the land, and more lately where she and her brothers had taken a loan for the seeds. Now, everything to do with the loans had fallen on her shoulders. This man, this Jace London, had said she was a *risk borrower,* but that he would take a chance on her if she put part of the farm up for collateral. In his words, it was all about collateral. Not knowing what else to do, she had done it.

The back three acres and two of the side acres became her "collateral"—five acres of prime farmland. She sighed. London must have found out that the soybeans drowned in the recent deluge. He must have known that when the rain didn't stop, their crop would have been destroyed—and she and her three brothers would be ruined.

Was he here to take the acres from her? To take the whole farm? To cancel the loans? She inhaled sharply, fearing what he might say.

"Stuart, tell him... Tell him I am busy."

Stuart shook his head. "I cannot lie. *Gott* would not want me to lie, Karen."

She put her hands heavily on his shoulders. "I am ... busy. And I'm tired, so it is not really a lie."

He blinked his big blue eyes. "It *is* a lie. You aren't too busy to talk. *Gott* says we are not to lie." He folded his arms in front of his chest.

She sighed with resignation. "All right. Tell him I will be right there."

She closed the door behind Stuart and put her back against it. Wringing her hands. *This is it. This is when I lose the farm, and we have nowhere else to live. Four orphans cast out onto the street. We will be at the mercy of someone to take us in. Oh, someone will want John, for sure, he is the eldest, and he can work hard. Everybody knows a seventeen-year-old is strong and able-bodied. Mark, too. He is only sixteen, but he could do a day's work like a twenty-year-old. But little frail Stuart, oh my, who would take care of my youngest brother? I could find a job, but I could not be with him during the day, and he certainly is not old enough to be on his own.*

Tears rolled down her cheeks. She shoved the heels of her hands up against her eyes, forcing the tears away. She heard a gentle tapping on the door. "Karen? It is John. The man is gone. I sent him away."

She opened the door. "What did you tell him?"

"I told him we would pay on time. I told him we are renting out rooms and will have the money to pay even though the rain killed much of the soybean crop. We will be all right, sister."

She stared at him. "Rent out rooms? To strangers?"

"*Jah*. We must do what we must do." He had more to tell her, but he was clearly not going to share the rest of his plan right now. His news would have to wait. "Come on, let's make some supper."

"Were you able to salvage at least some of the seedlings?"

He shook his head. "No soybeans this season, I'm afraid. Even if we get some more seeds and try to get them in the ground now, I fear it won't be a *gut* crop. It's late for planting."

She whispered, "Must there always be so much death, John? I am weary of so much death. People or plants, it is all death."

John towered above his older sister. He put his arm around her shoulders. "You were left with an impossible task. *Mamm* should never have asked for your promise to take care of all of us and the farm before she passed. It wasn't fair. You may be the eldest, but the truth is you are just..."

"Just one girl?" She tucked one of her curls back under her *kapp*, feeling a bit ashamed for behaving so badly. John had heard her promise *Mamm*. He must be feeling so much guilt when she demonstrated such bad behavior.

"I will be all right." She put on a smile. "Boarders, huh? All right. And how will we obtain those much-needed boarders?"

"I already put a note on the bulletin board outside the bakery and another one at the meat market. Someone will need a room. They will pay upfront and that will make up the payment we owe for the seeds, at least."

She could not help herself. "Seeds with no harvest. Just wasted money spent on seeds that will never produce. *Ach*, John, how will we ever survive? Why did *Mamm* die? She gave up on life, did she not? She left us with everything on our shoulders. Stuart is so young and Mark, too. We have to protect them."

She corrected herself. "*Nee*, I must protect them. *Mamm* told *me* to take care of the farm and all of you." She had not used the term *we* before in their struggles, not wanting to burden John, but he was seventeen, old enough to share the burden now.

He tightened his arm around her shoulders, "*Oh ye of little faith*. Everything is going to work out. You will see. Maybe you will meet a nice young man at the singing this weekend." He nudged her shoulder. "Never doubt that someday things will be *gut* again." He laughed softly. "When it is this bad, things must become *gut, ain't so?*"

"I don't know how things could get much worse. If only *Daed* had not taken out those other loans, I do believe we might have been able to do this. But the loans are such a heavy burden, even if the seedlings had made it, we would be in trouble." She thought for a moment. "We need to sell the buggy. It will bring in a *gut* price and the money is needed."

"The buggy? But how shall we all travel?" He stared into her anguished face.

"By pony cart. We will make do until we can buy another buggy—one day." She smiled. "We don't have to go to Sunday singing in a nice buggy." She gave him a brave smile, feeling better with her plan. "A buggy is not needed for us now. We can ill afford it. I usually ride in the pony cart, and so do you. I doubt you or I will even miss it."

John spoke slowly. "But Karen, *Daed* loved that buggy. That buggy was like our *daed's* right arm."

She bit her lower lip, "*Jah,* it is true. He liked driving the buggy." She took a gulp of air. "But *Daed* is dead."

They looked into each other's eyes. Neither said another word. The matter was settled. The buggy would be sold as soon as possible.

John turned to leave. "We can go over the books this evening and then make a solid plan for how we shall proceed. But for now, we need to eat. Will you come down to supper?"

"I'll get it on the table as soon as possible. We do have a roof and food." She wanted to add, *but for how long,* yet she knew John did not need any more reminders. She felt as if her heart would break every time she thought of her brothers having to work so hard on a farm they might lose. They never complained, but she knew how difficult it was; after all, she worked side-by-side with them most of the time plus took care of the household.

There was very little discussion at the supper table. They all knew if they did not get boarders, all was lost. There was not much to talk about.

Mark did try to make light conversation. "I think one of the hens is sitting on eggs we never collected. We will have chicks."

The continuous clinking of forks on plates echoed in the kitchen.

He tried again to get his siblings speaking. "Chicks can be sold and that's more money toward more seed or just toward any staples we might need. Do not everyone shout hurray at once."

Karen smiled, "It is a *gut* thing, Mark. But right now..."

A sharp knock on the kitchen door made all heads turn and stare. The door snapped open without anyone saying, "Come in."

"Hello, folks. Hope you do not mind. I made some cookies today and thought I would bring you some for your dessert. Now mind you, cooking is not my thing, but I like baking cookies well enough." Felix, the older widower smiled, his eyes crinkling at the corners. "I could not help but see on my walk over that your fields have been flooded. You're not the only ones around here it's happened to. I am sorry. And you lost the seedlings. If there is anything I can do..." he paused, then said quickly, "Here try the cookies."

He put the plate of cookies on the table and then turned to Karen. "I noticed one of your hens is sitting. You must have left the eggs. Chicks sell well in the spring. I mean, it's not much money, but every little bit will help."

"*Denki*, Felix." Karen motioned for him to sit. "I will get you a cup of tea. Are you hungry? Shall I make you a plate of food?"

"*Nee, denki*. I have eaten. I made a beef stew." He looked toward the stove and then leaned toward the brothers. "Boys, I could put on my waders and go out in the field with you tomorrow and maybe salvage some of the plants if you'd like some help."

The three boys shook their heads. John sighed. "Salvation is a lost cause, Felix. All the new baby shoots have drowned, but *denki* for offering."

"That is what neighbors are for. I always want to help. You boys know that." The man chewed on the side of his lip for a moment. Because he had been married previously, he had a long black beard which was streaked with gray.

He went on, "I don't think I have seen rain coming down so hard and so fast in a long time. A real gusher that storm." He chuckled, but then he glanced at the somber faces around the table. "Even the ducks at the pond had to bring out their little umbrellas. Never seen that." He laughed again.

No one laughed at his attempt at humor.

At times, Stuart had very little, if any, self-control. Now, he blurted, "The man from the loan bank came today and made Karen cry."

Felix immediately touched Karen's hand atop the table. "I am so sorry. Was he threatening to take the farm?"

Karen shot an angry glance at her youngest brother. "*Nee,* he gave us some more time. We have decided to take in boarders and also to sell the buggy. That will more than cover our payment for now."

Felix seemed uneasy in his chair, fidgeting with a napkin on the table. "Boarders? I see. Well, you never know what boarders are like, do you? I mean, they could be any type of person. I'm sorry it's come to this."

John shook his head. "I know, Felix, but taking in boarders is a necessary thing for our survival right now. We must open our home to strangers, *jah*. It is something we must do. We will be able to keep the farm."

"I read in *Die Botschaft*, just last week that someone came into a house and robbed an Amish home. They cut off the father's beard and were unkind to the women of the household, as well. Such is the dangerous world we live in. This is not like in the old days when there were *gut* people outside of the Amish circle, but now..."

John frowned in thought. "We can send a letter to the Amish newspaper. That newspaper reaches many Amish. They will print an advert for us for boarders."

Karen's eyes widened. She turned to Felix, "*Denki,* Felix. You always bring us *gut* ideas." She smiled at him.

John's forehead creased. "Uh, I thought it was my idea."

They all had a good laugh then, and Karen felt instantly better.

Felix watched Karen. He had always adored, maybe even loved, Karen, but of course, she did not know that fact. He knew the twenty-five years between them would make him seem ancient to her, beyond the ability to court her. He was well aware he should have his own grandchildren running all over his farm by now. But one could not have grandchildren without children, and one could not have children without a wife.

He also knew Karen would not consider him even remotely in line to be her husband, but then, there she was looking at him gratefully, which he could not ignore.

He spoke softly, "You're welcome, Karen." He looked into her eyes, hoping she could *see* his feelings for her. *Were not the eyes the windows of the soul?*

But she obviously saw nothing. She jumped up. "I shall go write a letter to send off to *Die Botschaft* right now. What a wonderful idea. There are surely people needing a room to rent."

Before Felix could make another comment, she hurried out of the kitchen.

Felix turned to the boys. "Your sister seems to be over-joyed with the prospect of strangers in your home. I hope it is a *gut* idea. Selling the buggy, well, *jah*, it will bring a *gut* price, but strangers ...?"

He had often admired the family's Helmuth buggy. Their father had chosen it well. The buggy was sturdy, and the black top even could be removed in the summer. It was a rare buggy, indeed. He felt sorry the family would have to part with it. Perhaps, he could make a bid on the buggy himself. "John, when will you put the buggy up for sale and for how much?" He ran his hand over his beard, imagining himself the new owner.

"We will need to discuss it. But ..." John scratched his head and gave Felix a figure. "It's in wonderful condition."

"Hmm. I could have a new buggy for that price," Felix said. Although, he wouldn't dicker over the price. He wanted to help the family—wanted to help Karen.

Mark shook his head. "It has deflectors all around and battery lights front and back with turn signals. Leather seats and a built-in gas heater. A *gut* family buggy."

"*Jah*, for me and my wife and *kinner*." Felix nodded.

Mark gaped at him. Everyone knew Felix's wife from his youth had died. Was the elder man delusional? Mark could not imagine Felix marrying anyone at this point. Yet, Felix wasn't all that old, he supposed. In fact, their district encouraged marriage for those who were widowed. Mark, who was much like Stuart, in-as-much-as he rarely guarded his words, stated bluntly, "Karen will not be fearful of having boarders. She is happy with the prospect of not starving out in the streets with us."

John slowly shook his head. "*Ach,* Mark. Too much talking. You and Stuart get to the dishes."

Mark watched Felix. The man obviously felt he was family. In truth, after their parents died, the neighbor had often stepped in to help on the farm, and he was there to give his advice, which was generally valued. Sometimes it was not solicited, but he was still a good friend.

"Felix, would you like to bring your tea into the living room? We could talk for a spell," John said.

Felix shook his head. "*Nee*, you are very kind, as always. But I shall head for home." He paused. "I do worry about your sister having so much on her shoulders. I know you boys help with the burden, but she appears to look so tired and worn lately, and now, with the loss of the crop, she seems defeated."

John sighed, the same weight of worry in his eyes. "Farming can take the life right out of us at times. The soybeans were one crop, but we have the others. Soon the wheat and then the corn."

He suspected Felix tried to make all conversations about Karen, but she had never given the man any cause to believe she was interested in him. He wanted Felix to know that Karen and the brothers were a solid family. They were a unit and worked together as a unit. They stuck together, and they worked out problems together, yet, as always, he did value the man's advice.

"Felix, I have something personal I want to discuss with you. May I walk with you outside?"

Felix stood. "Of course. I am always at the ready to help in any way that I can."

Felix's heart quickened. Maybe John knew he wanted to ask Karen to marry him. Of course, since John was the eldest brother, he would like to have his blessing. Maybe this was why the boy wanted to speak privately with him. Maybe John had seen how much he loved Karen. He tried to remain calm, but a smile formed uncontrollably on his lips. This was the moment he had hoped for, and now it was here.

Felix walked out of the kitchen ahead of John; then, the two walked side by side. John towered above him. Felix was trim for his age, though his stomach was a bit thick. He truly did not need his suspenders to keep up his pants, but of course, the suspenders were a part of his daily wear. He looked up at the young man.

"How can I help you, John?"

"What I am going to say may sound odd, but trust me, I have thought long and hard on this."

Hastily, Felix answered, "*Nee, nee,* nothing is crazy. I have an open mind. You know that about me." He struggled to keep his stride equal to John's. Felix's thoughts rushed through his mind. So the boy thought it crazy that he would want to marry, Karen, was that it? He held his breath. "Go on, tell me."

"Well, I am thinking about taking a job in the recreational vehicle factory over in Indiana. The job would pay me well, and I could send money home regularly. It is a *gut* job, steady."

Felix listened, and then he felt the raindrops starting to splat on his face. "Your secrecy is about a job? You want my advice about a job?"

"*Jah*. The job is in Indiana, but that is not too far to come back to the farm often. It pays very *gut* money to send home. I would not take the job forever, but until we can pull the farm out of its debts. What do you think?"

Felix wanted to say, *What do I think? I think I want to marry your sister, and then you will not have any concerns about money at all.*

But instead, he said, "Leave the farm when your sister needs your support so badly? You are the eldest brother. You are the one with strength to work the farm. Also, to leave her alone with boarders? *Nee,* John, how can this be a *gut* idea?"

John was clearly surprised by Felix's reaction. Usually, Felix was supportive of his ideas. He stopped walking. "I am still going to think about the job. It is just too much money for me to pass on. Karen could be out of trouble with the farm within months or a year or so with my pay being sent home. I ain't sure if we can sustain our lives without me leaving."

Felix did understand his urgency. "*Jah,* do more thinking and praying on this one. I'll check in tomorrow."

Felix nodded his farewell, slogging his way through the mud puddles on the way back to his own farm.

Chapter Two

The first boarder was an *Englischer*. Karen tried to dissuade the man, telling him he might be happier in a regular *Englisch* home, but he liked the fact that the room was cheaper than rooms in town.

"Mr. Olson, I—"

"Please call me Kevin."

"Kevin, I am thinking of you. I do not believe this room is a *gut* fit for an *Englischer*."

But Kevin was adamant. "I will take the room. I know what I'm doing." He eyed her suspiciously. "Just because I don't dress and act like you, you can't refuse me the room for rent. I know my rights."

Karen was taken aback. She knew nothing about *Englisch* law or rights. She truly was only concerned that he wouldn't be happy there. "You must be aware there is no electricity. None. There is no television or phone, everything you are accustomed to having. Amish eat and live differently. We have an old wringer washer—that is all. You must do your own laundry."

"I get it. Okay. I want the room."

She nodded then, giving up. "All right. It is yours."

"Thank you. I will take my laundry into town. I'll eat everything you eat. I do not see a problem. I keep to myself."

"The rent is due now for the month ahead."

He shrugged and handed her the cash.

"Follow me. Here is the bathroom which you will share with the family." She waited for his reaction, but he just nodded. "This is your room. I hope you find it acceptable."

"I lived in New York before here. I can adjust to anything." He grinned. He was not a handsome man, but he could have been, if his hair was combed and cut. His clothes were crumpled, like someone who had been traveling for long while. He had a stubble on his face from days without shaving.

She waved her hand in the air. "There is no need for a house key. We do not lock our doors. You may come and go as you need. Breakfast is at seven, the main meal at noon, and supper at six. If you have any questions, please, just ask. We do want you to be comfortable."

She closed her fingers tightly on the money he had just given her. The money would pay half a loan payment. She was breathing easier: a weight had been lifted. Maybe now things would begin to lighten up.

The second boarder who showed up at their door was Nicodemus Imhoff. He was an Amish gentleman newly arrived from Pennsylvania. He had just started his job as a clerk at the lumberyard in town. He had a nice, friendly smile and a comfortable look about him. She smiled to herself. *Well, my eyes are well-pleased, even if I daren't truly admit it.*

"Mr. Imhoff, your room is on the second floor at the end of the hall. Will that be all right with you?"

"Of course, it is all right with me. I will also want to participate in the district activities. I'm looking forward to making my home here. I also enjoy the youth singings."

"I'm sure you'll like them here. We have single people of all ages who attend. You may have to find transportation or ride in a pony cart. We may no longer have a buggy soon as we are considering selling ours."

"Fine, I can hire a car to take me if need be. My name is Nicodemus, and I prefer you call me that. When I hear you say, Mr. Imhoff, I find myself looking around for my *daed*." He grinned.

"Nicodemus, then."

His voice turned curious. "I saw your buggy in the yard, and it is a nice one. More on the expensive side, *jah*? I fear you will not get what it is worth, and it would be a shame to see it go. Of course, it ain't my business."

"In difficult times we do what we must do." She spoke softly, taking in his gentle tone and his consideration of her family. "So you work at the lumberyard?"

"*Jah*, it is what I could find for now. Times are difficult for everyone, but when we are resourceful, we can make it through." He smiled. "Resourceful like you, taking in boarders. That obviously is out of necessity, but *gut* thinking. I will go up to my room now. *Denki* for your help. Here is the first month rent." He reached in his pocket for the necessary cash. It was not wadded up like the *Englischer's* cash had been.

He started up the stairs, holding on to the railing with one hand and carrying his brown suitcase with the other. She watched him go up with strong deliberate steps. Nicodemus seemed like quite a decent fellow; she hoped she was right. She reminded herself to remain observant until she got to know him better.

Kevin came around the corner into the kitchen. "I don't understand why I can't get any signal out here. Yes, I know you don't have electricity, but I should get some type of signal. Why can't you run electricity to my room? Just one room, would that be such a big deal?"

Karen remained calm. "I'm sorry. That isn't permitted. I did tell you we are Amish, and we do not have electricity. You are welcome to utilize the electricity at the town's public library if you like. Maybe you should consider looking for another place for the next month."

"Naw, I don't want to live somewhere else. I like you people. I just don't like all your silly rules."

She shook her head. "We do live by certain rules." She smiled. "That is what makes us Amish."

Nicodemus had silently come down the stairs. "Is there anything I can help you with, Miss Helmuth?"

"Oh, *nee,* no trouble. This is our other boarder, Kevin. Kevin, this is Nicodemus."

Nicodemus eyed Kevin. "If you don't mind me asking, why would an *Englischer* decide to live way out in the country with the Amish?"

Kevin snorted. "I like it out here."

Karen reached for her purse on the bureau. "I have to go into town and pay a bill and get a few things. Do either of you need anything?"

Nicodemus took a step closer to her. "Miss Helmuth, may I drive you into town for your provisions, as I also need a few things, as well. It would be a shame to make you go alone."

Kevin laughed. "I thought you didn't drive. Do you have a car or something?"

"I was meaning I shall drive the buggy if Miss Helmuth wishes me to." He smiled at Karen. "May I accompany you?"

"I suppose it would be nice to have company. *Denki,* Mr. Imh —, uh, Nicodemus."

"I will go and hitch up the horse while you get ready and prepare your own list of items." He nodded to Kevin. "Pleasure to meet you, Kevin."

Karen didn't know why she had agreed to allow Nicodemus to drive her to town. She felt awkward sitting on the bench seat with him. He was quite proper, that was not the issue, and he was certainly an excellent buggy driver. But they rode in silence for most of the way there.

Quite unexpectedly he said, "I once leased a farm. I gave it up due to a tornado twisting right through the barn and then the house. I could have stayed and tried to rebuild with the owner, but I needed a change of scene." He smiled. "Sometimes *Gott* pushes us in new directions."

She watched his hands as he gently moved the reins. He did know what he was doing, and the horse responded in kind. She ventured, "Farming can be hard. My brothers and I are doing the best we can, but it does seem sometimes *Gott* has other plans for us, as well."

A horse and buggy were coming toward them on the other side of the road.

"Hello." It was Felix and he was looking at her with great curiosity. He didn't look pleased. "Where are you going, Karen?"

"Felix, hello, this is Nicodemus Imhoff, our new boarder. We are going to town for some supplies, and I am going to pay some bills."

Felix's eyes narrowed very slightly, and he halted his horse right next to the buggy driver. "Where are you from Nicodemus?"

"Lancaster." Nicodemus did not smile at Felix, nor did he sound overly friendly. "Miss Helmuth and I must hurry before the stores close. Pleasure to meet you."

Felix did not move. "How did you learn about the rooms for rent?" he asked in a level voice.

"What difference does it make?" Karen asked, trying to infuse a lightness to the conversation. "He's here now."

"I was just wondering..." Felix said.

Karen was puzzled. Why did he seem so upset? He had known they were going to rent out rooms.

"Now we have to be moving along," she said.

Nicodemus nodded and snapped the reins, to which, the horse immediately responded.

Felix sat quietly on his horse watching the buggy pull away. He felt a strange feeling roll through his body, a feeling which he hadn't felt for years. His face burned hot. His hands twitched. He was jealous because another man was sitting next to Karen riding into town. He wanted to turn his horse around to follow them, to watch over her with this stranger, whoever he was.

"I'm sorry, Nicodemus. Felix has always felt a little protective of our family. We have been neighbors since before our parents passed. I suppose Felix feels a sense of responsibility toward us."

"No need to apologize for the man. He seemed to over-step his boundaries a bit, but I am sure he was just being a protective neighbor. After all, he had not met me yet. Yet, there does seem a possessiveness about him. Like someone who is keeping watch over his own daughter or wife."

Karen did not say a word, but her mind was racing. She had never seen Felix's face so flushed; even his voice was edgy, like he might jump right into the buggy and take the reins from Nicodemus. She was glad Nicodemus was so calm and handled the moment, but it was awkward. Maybe Nicodemus was right—did Felix feel like he somehow had a some kind of authority over her?

She smiled. "I must go into this loan company here."

Nicodemus nodded. "Oh, at this bank. I know banks make loans."

"My brothers and I had to continue to do business with these people since no one else was interested after our parents died. It is a long story." She spoke quietly, suddenly trusting him with their family secrets. "*Daed* borrowed money, actually two loans, and my brothers and I also borrowed for the seeds which now, unfortunately, have all perished in the rain. We thought we were doing the right thing, but it seems once a family is in a downward financial spiral, well, it just keeps going downward."

Nicodemus's brow creased. "Three loans? *Ach,* that is a lot."

"You and Kevin are helping with your rent payments, and of course, we will have more crops soon and my brother, John, works for others when he can. He is actually a *gut* carpenter. Mark also picks up odd jobs."

Nicodemus shook his head. "I will help when I can on the farm. I can plow and I can..."

"*Nee*, that is not necessary. You pay your rent and that is help enough."

He jumped down from the bench seat and offered his hand to help her down. "You must be burdened with so much responsibility. I want to help."

She wondered at herself. Why in the world had she shared so much with him? It was unseemly, wasn't it? She wished she had kept her family's story to herself. And then she wondered whether if he left his hand on hers longer than he needed to when he helped her down.

"I-I am not too burdened. Things will get better soon. And now we have two boarders."

"*Jah*, well, I am going to help you when and where I can. I know what it is like to fight to keep a farm. I lost my fight. Now, I punch a clock and work for others, and it is all right, I s'pose. I make a wage. I do my best, and this is *gut* enough for me."

She could hear the pain in his voice. He may have said it was good enough, but he was not convincing.

He went on. "I keep thinking that if I can just save enough money, I can buy a farm of my own this time."

"I understand." She turned toward the loan building. "I have to go in here. I won't be long."

"And it is high interest, I don't doubt. These types of places often hurt their borrowers with high rates."

She nodded, "He has our loan at twelve percent."

"*Ach*." He shook his head. "This should never be. Should I go in with you?"

"*Nee*. Stay here." She hurried into the building, now wishing more than ever that she hadn't said a word. Imagine a stranger coming in with her while she paid her family's debt.

Immediately, she spotted Jace London sitting at his desk. He rose to greet her. "Hello, Karen. I have not seen you in too long. Usually John comes in to pay. This is a pleasant surprise. How are you? How are things at the farm? Were you able to salvage any plants or are you building an ark?"

She acknowledged his joke with a forced smile. She did not sit but handed him the minimum amount due. "A receipt, please."

"Of course. Of course. Just have a seat and I'll print one after I count this." He began to count the bills. "You seem to be twenty dollars short. I will use the machine this time."

She shook her head, "*Nee*, it is exact. I counted it several times before I came in."

He fed the money into the machine. "There, you see, short twenty dollars."

She shook her head again, bewildered. "The money was all there when I handed it to you, Mr. London. I promise you that. Please, can you count it again?"

"I'm so sorry, but you are twenty short."

Her shoulders fell. How could she have made such a foolish mistake? "I'm sorry."

He shrugged. "Do you have the money? As you know, we aren't too excited about partial payments. Particularly when you're late."

"Let me go look outside. Maybe I dropped it."

He handed her back the money. "I am sorry, Miss Helmuth. All or nothing. We've been very lenient with you in the past."

She rushed out to the buggy. "Nicodemus, it seems I am twenty dollars short, and I knew I had it when I put it in my bag. Could you help me look? I may have dropped it on the ground or in the buggy or..."

Nicodemus searched the area around the bench seat and jumped down and looked around the buggy. He looked along the sidewalk and in the gutter. "Give me the money, Karen, I will go in and pay the man. What is his name?"

She did not argue this time, but immediately handed him the money. "His name is Jace London."

He nodded. "Here, let me help you up into the buggy. I know you had the money, Karen, I saw you count it." He helped her back onto the bench seat.

Jace London looked up at the stranger in front of his desk, "May I help you?"

"*Jah*. Miss Helmuth came in to pay with all her money in hand, and then you told her that she did not have enough. Is that correct?"

"And you are...?"

"A friend. Can you kindly count the money again?"

"I feel really badly about this. I've counted it more than once. It's twenty short."

"Please. One more time."

Jace put the money into a machine that counted it with the same result. "I'm sorry."

Nicodemus pulled a twenty from his own pocket and added it to the amount. "There. It's correct now, *ain't so?*"

Jace smiled at him. "It is at that. I'll print a receipt." The machine beside him whirred. "Here you are."

"*Denki*, Mr. London. We appreciate it."

"Did he find my twenty dollars?" Karen asked when Nicodemus returned.

"It was all fine," Nicodemus said, not elaborating on what happened. He didn't want Karen feeling beholden to him.

She looked at him gratefully and took the receipt and put it in her bag. They bought their supplies and headed back to the farm. Nicodemus couldn't help himself. On the ride home, he inched a bit closer to her on the bench seat. He hoped she wouldn't notice, but for him it was worth the risk. She was so sweet, so innocent, yet so strong. His heart warmed with the very thought of her.

Chapter Three

Dear Journal,

I am at a loss. John continues to talk about the need to go to Indiana to work at the RV plant. I know it is only Indiana, but I cannot bear for him to go. I cannot imagine how I will manage the farm without him. It is rather selfish of me, I know, but I need him. Jah, there will be more money, but there will be no John to help with the heavy things, like baling or scything.

The boarders are working out. Even Kevin seems to be complaining less, and that is a huge blessing for which I'm grateful. He still grumps about the conveniences not being here, but he is adjusting. Nicodemus has proven himself as a kind, gut man. He even helped me do some gardening the other day. He is always considerate and generous.

I think—well, I should not think these thoughts, but I do have them. I think he will make someone a gut husband one day. Not that I am thinking these thoughts for myself. I have no time for courting, although Felix has expressed interest in marrying me. I was stunned the first time he brought it up. He has jumped right over talking with John and now just continues to ask me every chance he finds me alone.

But he is so much older than me. In truth, many Amish women have married an older man, but I never thought of myself doing so. I put him off, and it pains me to see the disappointment in his eyes. Still, I do not love him—at least not in that way.

My brother Stuart is not feeling well tonight. He did not eat his supper. Oh, I wish Mamm *was here. She always knew how to take care of us when we were ill. There were so many things I wanted her to teach me, things only a* mamm *can teach her daughter. I miss* Mamm *and* Daed *so much, especially now. There are days I just don't know what I am going to do. We have loans we must pay back, or the farm will be taken from us. The bank man was cold and harsh to me today. Nicodemus took care of it for me. He is proving to be not only a decent boarder, but a very kind and* gut *friend.*

P.S. I keep telling John not to go to Indiana. I do not know how much longer we can hold on financially, but I pray he does not leave me alone to handle the farm.

A light tapping on her bedroom door made Karen finish her journal entry quickly. She had been keeping a journal since not long after she learned how to write. At first, the journal gave her practice with her spelling and penmanship, but more importantly, it got all her thoughts out on paper. After her parents' death, writing in her journal somehow eased the difficulties of her life.

Now, she asked, "*Jah*, who is it?"

"John."

She went to the door and opened it. "What is it?"

"Stuart has taken a turn for the worse. He's muttering nonsense now. We may need the herbal woman, or I fear, a doctor."

Karen rushed past her brother, even though she was only in her flannel nightgown. She hurried to Stuart's room. "John, bring a bowl of cool water and a cloth. And bring the vapor rub." She remembered her *mamm* had always used vapor rub.

In the lantern light, Stuart tossed back and forth in his bed. The sheets were damp from his hot sweating body. He even appeared thinner than usual. She brushed his sandy hair back from his forehead and put the cool cloth on his head.

"Stuart, can you hear me? I'm here. We'll help you."

He continued to moan and move back and forth until John came back into the room.

"John, I fear you're right. This is beyond the herbal woman. Go get the buggy. We have to get him to the doctor."

John hurried to the door and then turned back abruptly. "How will we pay?"

She swallowed. "We will use the savings."

"There aren't savings, and you know it, Karen. The only money we have is for next month's loan payments."

"We must use it. Please don't argue. Get the buggy."

He stepped back to her and touched her shoulder. "I'll get the buggy. But I'm telling you right now, I am going to Indiana. We cannot live like this. Not when I can help by leaving."

She shivered. "We'll talk later. Get the buggy and then help me get Stuart into it."

Karen pulled the light quilt up to Stuart's chin to wait till the buggy was hitched. John was right about everything. But oh, the thought of him leaving just about did her in. From behind her, she heard a familiar voice.

"I'll stay with Stuart while you get dressed." Nicodemus said at the doorway. "He will be all right. Don't worry. I will carry him to the buggy."

She gave a start. "*Ach*, I didn't hear you."

"I'm sorry. I didn't mean to alarm you. I heard the ruckus. Let me help."

"*Denki*, Nicodemus." She rushed out of the room. The man was so dependable, so strong and steadfast. She felt tears welling in her eyes. *Why doesn't Nicodemus ask to court me? He seems the perfect man. He has such a kind heart.*

John drove the buggy to the hospital where the doctor was adamant that Stuart must be hospitalized for tests. Karen watched in horror when the nurse put the oxygen mask on her little brother's face.

"Is he going to be all right? Is he … going to die?" Her voice was weak and shaking. She had seen her *daed* die. She had seen her *mamm* die, and she could not bear the thought of losing little Stuart.

"We'll do everything we can," said the nurse.

"Please help my little brother. Please." Tears rolled down her cheeks. She took his limp hand in hers. "Oh, dear *Gott*, please do not let Stuart die, too," she prayed silently.

The Lord sustains him on his sickbed; in his illness you restore him to full health. The verse from the psalms rang through her mind. She had to believe God would spare Stuart.

She sat in the small waiting room outside of Stuart's hospital room. John had returned to the farm to let them know what was going on and to start the chores. Nicodemus had excused himself to see if he could find some coffee.

Karen heard sharp footsteps coming toward her, "Miss Helmuth?"

"*Jah?*" The fear tasted bitter in her mouth. *Was this the dreaded moment to hear those horrible words she had heard twice before?* She began to shake.

"I am Doctor Rosen. I need your consent to operate on Stuart. His appendix has become enlarged, and we must remove it immediately. It is a fairly common procedure, and he should be fine. The appendix has not ruptured. You brought him in just in time."

She could not say the words fast enough. "*Jah, jah*, you have my consent, of course."

She signed the papers and watched them wheel Stuart off to the operating room. She began to cry softly. The words she had prayed for, rang over and over in her ears. *He should be fine. He should be fine...*

That was all that mattered now. If she had to, she would sell the farm. She would find them an apartment and she would work in a store or a bakery. John could work in Indiana and send money to help, and Mark was old enough to work, too. They would figure everything out. Nothing mattered more than her little brother's life.

"Karen?" She lifted her head to look into Nicodemus' eyes. He offered her a cup of coffee. "Are you all right, *liebling?*"

She closed her eyes. *Had he just called her darling?* Her heart leapt. Maybe Nicodemus would be the one. Maybe he would ask her to marry him, and then everything would be all right.

She shook her head and shuddered. She was tired and her mind was going places it shouldn't.

"*Jah,* I am all right. Stuart had..."

"I know. I spoke with one of the nurses. He will be fine now. An appendectomy." Nicodemus smiled. "In a few days, he will be as *gut* as new."

Within seconds, Felix entered the waiting room. He carried a small bag of cookies. "Is everything okay? Is Stuart going to be all right?"

Karen smiled, "He is in surgery, and he will recover. It's his appendix. *Denki* for coming, Felix."

"Of course. I must come. I am like family. I brought cookies." He held the bag out to them. "I didn't bake them this time. I picked them up at the bakery this morning on my way in. I think they are *gut,* but..." He glanced at Nicodemus with a surprised look. "You are here?" Was Karen mistaken, or did that almost sound like an accusation? "I can take over now. You may go about your business."

Karen touched his arm. "It's all right, Felix. Nicodemus can stay. He has been helping me."

Felix sat on the other side of her on the small vinyl couch. He took her hand in his and squeezed it. "You must have been so frightened. Thank *Gott* you arrived at the hospital in time. A bad appendix can be deadly."

"We got him here by buggy, but *jah,* thank *Gott,* we were in time."

"The surgery will cost..." Felix started, and his brow furrowed.

Nicodemus shook his head, "Don't worry Karen about expenses now. It'll be all right."

Felix nodded, "*Jah,* we shall worry about all those things later."

Karen was feeling awkward sitting between the two men who seemed to be sparring, though she couldn't think why. Her mind was totally consumed with her brother. The minutes ticked by. The three of them stared straight ahead, and no one spoke now, as they waited for the doctor.

Finally, Nicodemus asked, "May I get you a hot tea? You're finished with your coffee."

"Tea would be nice," Karen said.

He smiled and hurried off.

Felix was frowning now. "He seems to be around you a lot. And he seems to have uh, well, feelings for you."

In a tired voice, she responded, "He is a friend, Felix. A friend."

"Have you given any more thought to marrying me, Karen? All your troubles could be over. I am a man of some means, as you know, and I can take care of you and your brothers. You would not have to worry about the farm being sold or about these hospital bills. Please allow me to take these worries from you."

"*Ach,* Felix, please. I can't discuss this now."

"After Stuart recovers, then we will talk. I do love you, Karen. I love you with all my heart. I would be a *gut* husband. I may be older, but..." He stopped. "I'm sorry. Later. We'll talk later."

She cocked her head to one side to look deeply into his eyes. He was a kind man—a good man. She simply didn't have it in her right then to truly consider his words.

At that moment, Nicodemus came down the hall with a cup in his hands. "Nice and hot, our Karen. Be careful when you sip."

Felix's eyebrow shot up at the word, *our.* He said, "Shouldn't you be returning home, Nicodemus? Don't you have a job to go to?"

Nicodemus glanced at him but didn't respond. He looked back at Karen. "I will call into my job from the phone shanty. I have sick days, and I can stay here with you."

"*Nee,* you go to work, Nicodemus. You will need your full paycheck."

"I have three days paid sick leave."

She shook her head, "*Nee,* go to your work. Jobs are difficult to come by nowadays. You don't want to get fired."

He looked from her to Felix and back again. "Are you staying with her, Felix?"

"If she needs me, *jah*. I'd like to stay." Felix was looking at her now.

"Both of you, go home. I am fine." She put her hands on her knees.

Felix nodded to Nicodemus. "I will stay with her and take her home in my buggy when she is ready."

Nicodemus leaned toward Karen. "Will you be all right? I can stay."

"I'll see you later, Nicodemus. Go now."

Nicodemus walked quietly away. He feared that Felix might be chosen as the better man for Karen. After all, Felix owned a farm. He likely had savings. He was not a boarder working as a checker.

Nicodemus understood basic economics. Karen was in a financial corner, and anyone cornered, person or animal, fought for their survival. He whispered, "I am not even a contender in this. She would be a fool to choose me. Yet, Karen could be my helper. I am sure of it, and I could be hers. We'd find a way to make more money. Besides, *Gott* takes care of the birds and he..."

Nicodemus hurried down the long stairwell of the hospital. So many steps, but there was no reason to take the elevator. There was no emergency now. By the time he was on the last step, he was out of breath. He saw Felix's buggy parked at the back of the hospital parking lot.

Just seeing the buggy made him lament out loud, "I don't even have a buggy to take her for a ride or to just take her home from the hospital."

He sighed. He had to figure out a way to make money so she would realize he was ambitious and willing to work hard for what he wanted. *From the lowly can come great things, and Karen is not one to just weigh things by appearances alone. She will weigh my merits as to who I am.*

He strolled over to Felix's buggy. It was fine. Not as nice as the one Karen and her brothers were planning to sell, but a good buggy. Nicodemus put his hand against the door and gave it a quick slap. He was not about to let monetary things get in his way of marrying Karen Helmuth.

He slapped the door again, "Nothing. Nothing between Karen and me."

Chapter Four

Karen and Felix walked side by side as they left the hospital. She was fretting. "I don't like leaving Stuart here by himself. Suppose he needs me?"

Felix sighed. "There is nothing you can do right now. Besides, the nurses are very *gut*. He will have his own nurse until he can get up and walk properly. Normally, these days, an appendix operation recovery is very quick."

"Is this my fault because I delayed bringing him to a doctor?" Karen asked, feeling the weight of guilt fill her.

"*Nee*. You are a *gut* sister. When your parents died, you rose to fill their shoes. You did not even let yourself grieve properly. I saw that. You were there for your brothers, and they came first, just as your *mamm* would have wanted. Please relax, Karen. The doctors will keep Stuart a couple days, and then we can bring him home. He will be fine. I am just happy that I stayed at the hospital, so I am able to drive you back."

He helped her up onto the bench seat.

"Here, this quilt over your knees is a requirement. It is getting chilly in the evenings. You have had quite the ordeal, and I am sure you are exhausted."

She let him tuck the blanket around her knees. They had not ridden very far when her head began to bounce and bob, as she nodded off to sleep. Finally, her head plopped down against his shoulder, and she fell into a deep sleep.

He murmured over her black outer *kapp*, "Ah, *jah*. This is *gut*. Rest *liebling. Jah*." He wanted to put his arm protectively around her, but he knew it would be too forward. He contented himself with her sleeping head on his shoulder.

Karen would have slept all the way to the farm, but a scraping sound pierced the air, waking her up, just as the buggy started around a corner. Felix thought it was the sound of the change in the asphalt on the road, but the front wheels wobbled, and the buggy began to tip.

Karen screamed as the buggy fell to one side, smashing into a ditch.

Felix was thrown from the buggy and landed with a jolting thud, and everything went black.

Karen squirmed her way out of the buggy and stood as if in a daze. Then she noticed the horse struggling to get up, and she hurried over to set it loose with shaking hands. She shuddered, and then she remembered Felix.

"Felix," she cried, frantically searching the area. Her breath caught as she saw him lying by the side of the road. She rushed to him and wept with relief when she saw he was still breathing. But he was unconscious. She wriggled out of her coat and wrapped it around him.

"I'm going for help," she told him through her tears. "I'll be back as soon as I can."

Feeling disoriented, she started down the deserted road. She had to get help and fast. Where was she exactly? What farm was near? She tried to shake the fog from her mind. Confused, she looked up and down the road and couldn't place anything.

"Keep walking," she ordered herself. "You've got to find help. Keep walking."

And so she did, but her legs hurt, and she wasn't at all sure she was going the right way.

Back at the farm, no one was expecting Karen home that night. She had said she was going to stay with Stuart. No one knew she had changed her mind at Felix's coaxing. And Stuart had told her groggily she did not need to coddle him. No one was anticipating her arrival; so no one was going to search for her.

Nicodemus dried the last dish and put it back on the shelf. Mark had proven a fast dishwasher and completed the job in no time, leaving his kitchen partner alone to finish drying and putting away the dishes. Try as he might, Nicodemus could not get Karen out of his mind. He knew he had fallen in love with her, but he had nothing to offer. What could a man with no home offer a woman who had a home and a family? Had he anything to offer to such a wonderful woman? Absolutely nothing. He muttered, "I only have my love. Will it be enough?"

John stood in the kitchen doorway. "Who are you talking to, Nico?" John had started to call the boarder by the nickname some days back. Nicodemus was even getting used to the new name, and he liked the familiarity between the two of them. *Could he confide in the older brother? Could he tell him the truth?*

"I ... uh, I have a problem."

"What problem could you have? You have very little responsibility, except paying your rent, and beyond that, you are a free man." John chuckled. "There is a lot to say about being a free man."

"*Nee,* I have a true problem. Can I confide in you?"

John was curious. "Is this about my sister? Somehow, I think it is. You won't be the first to tell me she is your problem."

Nicodemus frowned. "She works tirelessly for this family. She is the pillar you all depend on." His voice turned tense. "So someone else has sought your advice about your sister?"

"Oh, dear Lord, do not tell me you are also sweet on my sister."

Nicodemus's frown deepened. "I am. But I have nothing to offer her."

John sighed heavily. "Nico, you are a nice man, a caring man and I am sure if you can establish yourself, it would be all right, but as it stands, *nee*. Thanks to my *mamm's* last words to her, my sister has the yoke of the farm around her neck and feels as if she must be the head of this family with three brothers to fret over. Why would she even think of marrying someone who is a boarder in her home with nothing of his own?"

His words sent an arrow to Nicodemus' heart. "But I am saving my money. I have plans to open my own shop and to build up my own business. Even to own a farm again."

"*Jah* and that takes time, Nico. Time is one thing my sister does not have. As it is, I am taking the job in Indiana. She does not even know it for sure yet, but I have to do my fair share so we can keep this farm in the family." He shook his head, "I'm sorry. I don't mean to hurt you, but I must be truthful."

"If I spoke to her, and she heard my sincere plans..."

"Well, you can always try to convince her, but I doubt if she is able to wait at this point. Her only saving grace will be to find someone to marry who can help her manage the debt of the farm and, of course, all the work the farm entails. I am sure you understand. I'll be sending money home, but there will still be many worries on her shoulders. By leaving, I'm trying to protect her as best I can."

Nicodemus reluctantly nodded. He wanted to say, *And protect your own interest in the farm at the same time,* but he did not say it. His frustration was not going to change a single thing. He went to the kitchen door; he did not tell John he was planning on taking the buggy to go to the hospital. He had to speak with Karen. He had to let her know how much he cared. Then, if she rebuffed him, he would accept her answer.

John stepped forward and placed his hand on Nicodemus's arm, "I can tell you are planning to go there tonight, Nico. Prepare your heart for the pain of another sharp arrow. I know Karen cannot accept your courtship. There is no future in it."

"I'm going to try."

John nodded, "I know. Go if you must. It is all in *Gott's* hands, anyway."

Nicodemus did not force the horse to trot. The road was slippery from the rain, and he didn't want to risk the horse slipping. He tried to keep him on the shoulder of the road, where his hooves could grip the earth. He didn't know if it was some type of inner feeling, or if he saw the scene first, but when he saw the upturned buggy his heart lurched, and he knew it was Felix's. At first, he couldn't comprehend what he was seeing. And then, he cupped his hands to his mouth, "Karen! Karen Helmuth."

A male voice responded, "I'm here. Hey, over here."

Nicodemus knew that voice. It was Felix Sutter.

Chapter Five

Within an hour, dozens of Amish were searching for Karen. Felix was recuperating at his farmhouse, but the herbal woman and the doctor who had come felt he would be fine. Miraculously, he had no broken bones, just many bruises and a slight case of hyperthermia. He refused bedrest and wanted to go out searching for Karen with everyone else. The doctor had insisted that a nurse stay with him with strict orders that he not leave.

John, Mark, and Nicodemus walked along the banks of the river, shouting Karen's name. They walked the path downstream, fearing that somehow she might have fallen into the river which ran beside the road. They crawled over boulders, holding onto branches that dipped into the water, yelling for her over and over.

Before early morning, John put his arm around Mark's shoulders. "We might have to wait and see if her..., if she..." He could not finish as hot tears ran down his cheeks. His younger brother, who had been so stoic and brave, also began to weep. Nicodemus watched helplessly as the boys fretted in their grief.

Nicodemus shook his head. "We have to keep going. Your sister would not quit. She is here somewhere. Maybe she is recuperating in someone's home right now."

"She would have sent word," John said. "She'd know we would be looking for her."

The three of them continued searching, craning their eyes along the river's edge, seeking any clue that their sister might have come this way. Mark began to call out again, "Karen! Karen!" The others also began to shout with renewed energy.

Then, where the river took a bend right before the rapids, they saw a heap of clothes along the bank. Mark squinted. "There! I see something!"

They began to scramble recklessly over the rocks, slipping and hitting their knees, and righting themselves again, not even acknowledging their pain. Nicodemus shouted, "It is her clothes!"

But once they got to the heap, they realized that the heap of clothes was actually their sister, curled into a tight ball. Her body was battered and bruised, and even in the shadows, her face was a faint blue, but not yet as blue as her lips. She was shivering uncontrollably.

John removed his jacket quickly and rolled it around her. Mark did the same and he held her close. Nicodemus whispered, "Gently, gently, hold her gently. She might be badly hurt."

He wanted to hold her in his arms and give her all his warmth, but he watched helplessly as her brothers tended to her.

Mark, who was the fastest, began to scramble to his feet. "I will get help. You stay with her."

John and Nicodemus watched him leaping from rock to rock. John called out, "Be careful, Mark."

Karen was transported to the hospital emergency room. She was cognizant enough to fight it, but she had to acquiesce. She was placed in the Intensive Care Unit, and none of them were allowed in to see her until she was stabilized.

John told Stuart what had happened, and Stuart wept when he heard.

John and Mark stood under the bright overhead lights of the hospital hallway. Doctors and nurses bustled to and fro. Nicodemus stood in a corner watching them. He had not heard any of the reports of how Karen was, but he felt the brothers would tell him in due time. John saw him, and he and Mark went over to him.

"Nicodemus, *denki* for helping us find her. We do not know yet exactly how she is, but the doctors say she is a very lucky girl."

Nicodemus' head dropped to his chest. "Her face was blue. So blue and cold."

John nodded. "*Jah*."

They went to see Stuart. As they entered his room, he began to cry again. Nicodemus put his arm around the young boy. Ten was allowed to cry. Ten years in the world and so much sadness, so much pain. If only Nicodemus had the power to help the family, but the only thing to do now was to pray.

"Let's pray. *Gott* will hear our pleas. He helped us find her. He will help us by getting her well."

The brothers prayed with Stuart and then followed Nicodemus into the small sitting room. John closed the door. "Nicodemus, you keep saying that she is a fighter. You were right. *Denki* to *Gott* we did not give up our search."

Nicodemus smiled at the brothers before him. "*For where two or three are gathered together in my name, there am I in the midst of them.* Matt. 18:19–20." They then prayed again silently, hoping that *Gott* would send them a miracle for Karen.

Back at Felix's farmhouse, when he was told by his nurse that they had found Karen, he began to dress to leave.

"But Mr. Sutter, she cannot have visitors. They don't know how she is. She is in intensive care. Her brothers are at the hospital with her, and I promise to update you on her condition."

"*Nee.* That is not *gut* enough for me. Please leave my room while I dress. I will fetch my horse and go to her and her brothers. We are family. Do you understand, nurse? *Family.* Family must be together during times like this."

"But Mr. Sutter—"

He gently pushed her out of his room with his hands firmly on her back. He shut the door behind her and raised his voice so she could still hear him. "I will go to Karen. I must be there to support my family."

Nicodemus and the brothers were surprised to see Felix opening the sitting room door. He saw them with their heads bowed and jumped to a conclusion. "Oh, dear *Gott*, Karen has died. *Nee, nee.*" He fell to a chair, his eyes filled with tears.

John got up quickly and put his arm around the older man's shoulders, "*Nee, nee,* she is still with us, Felix. She is strong. We are praying."

Felix's tears turned to those of relief. Nicodemus stood. "We have to have faith. It's going to be all right. It has to be. We are praying for a miracle."

Felix gulped at the air. "*Jah*, a miracle for my Karen. I don't know what happened to that buggy. How could this happen?"

John made eye contact with his brother. Now all of them knew Felix loved their sister. They looked upon the older man with compassion. They knew in their hearts that given a choice, Felix would not be the man their sister would choose to marry.

Chapter Six

Dear Journal,

I was in the hospital for too long, but here I am, home again. The boys are so gut to me, always waiting on me. Granted, I have my arm broken—not my writing arm, and my leg is broken in two places. John will not let me have a mirror to see my face, but by the pain in my cheeks, I can imagine that I do not look so appetizing when I am sitting at the kitchen table. John half carries me to the table for my meals. The herbal woman comes to help bathe me. I am like some kind of baby. I need to heal quickly as John will soon be gone. He says he must go to Indiana.

She paused in her writing and stared at the window. It was raining. It had been raining for days.

She began to write again:

Too much rain. The final dose to drown anything that might have bravely peeked its little green head up. Definitely no crop of soybeans this year. John leaves this weekend for Indiana. He did not give any option to me, just said that was that. He said the farm could not be worked anyhow with all the rain. True. So Mark and Stuart can handle the milking, and once things dry out...

A knock at her bedroom door stopped her writing again.

"Karen, there's someone here to see you."

Stuart had grown so much during this ordeal. She saw it in his face and heard it in his voice. He was no longer the impatient little ten-year-old he had been before the accident. She was sad for that. A ten-year-old should be able to be his age instead of growing up to take care of his older sister.

"Who is it?" she asked.

"That loan guy, Jace London. Mark is out there with him."

Karen said, "I will see him. Take him into the living room, then come back to help me."

She struggled to sit in the bed, managing to put on a clean white apron over her gray dress. She straightened her *kapp*. She leaned over to open the drawer and took out the money for the loans—the money that Nicodemus and Kevin had given her for the month. She rolled it all together and secured it tightly with a rubber band.

Mark helped her up. She grumbled, "I think I can walk with your help. I do not know why you have to practically carry me."

"*Nee,* the doctor says no weight on your foot until next week. Be a *gut* patient, please. Besides, you are as light as a feather."

It was true. Karen had lost quite a bit of weight and Mark had grown stronger with the ever-present physical work of the farm. Like Stuart, he had also changed. Both of her younger brothers had suddenly become her equals, leaping over hurdles of years of growth. Fearing she was dead, searching for her in the boulders along a wild river had done that to her brothers. They were no longer the *kinner* she thought they were—now *she* was the *kinner.* The realization stung.

"I am not a little girl, you know. You boys could go and help poor John."

Mark shook his head. "He said he wanted to be alone. I think he is sad about leaving. He just wants to work it all through."

"I think so, too. He doesn't want to go to Indiana, I know that, but he feels he must so he can send money to pay off the debts." Normally, she would never discuss the financial business with young Mark, but he did not seem young anymore. He helped her like a man. He talked to her like a man.

Jace London was sitting in a high-back wooden chair. He stood when Mark entered the room supporting Karen. Mark

KEEPING THE FAMILY TOGETHER

gently helped her to the sofa. "Good to see you, Karen. However, I am so sorry about your injuries."

"*Denki* for coming here, Mr. London. I could not get to the bank, as you can see, but here is the money." She held out her hand. He reached for it, counted it, and quickly placed the rolled money into his pocket.

"This is not our normal procedure, of course," he said to her kindly. "Making house calls. But given all that your family has gone through recently, I decided breaking with our usual protocol would be in order. Besides, it is a small town. These kinds of things happen in small towns."

"Receipt?" She leaned her head back as a pain shot through her leg.

"My receipt book is in the car. If you will excuse me, I will go get it."

Expediently, she asked, "Mark, can you go to Mr. London's car and get his receipt book, please?" After the discrepancy with the twenty dollars, she couldn't quite make herself trust the man. She certainly insisted on a receipt.

"I will." Mark had been leaning up against the wall, watching the man closely.

"It's on the front seat, passenger side. I can't think why I didn't bring it in with me."

The man's car was unlocked. Mark snapped open the door. He put his hands on the seat, feeling the rich leather under his palms. He sniffed. He smelled a mix of leather and men's cologne. He closed his eyes a moment and imagined how it would feel to drive a car like this, to go soaring down the road at high speeds, passing all the Amish wagons and buggies. He stared at the shift knob and looked into the mirror.

"I'd like a car like this," he announced to his reflection. He was shocked when the thought came tumbling out of his mouth. He quickly reached for the pink receipt book lying on the passenger seat. As he backed out of the car, he heard a voice say, "Like fancy cars do you, Mark?" Nicodemus moved out of the way, so the car door could open all the way.

"*Jah*, it is a nice one. One of those things the *Englischers* have that sometimes makes me yearn. All the leather inside and all. A truly nice car. I was just getting the receipt book for that bank guy."

"That bank guy is here *again*? This is *his* car?" Nicodemus looked toward the front door and then back at the luxury car. "I'm sorry to know that man is here."

Mark nodded, "Poor Karen, with all her pain and having to deal with this guy, but John is in the field and..."

"*Jah*, well, if she would marry me, I would take care of that bank business."

"Would you, now, Nico? And how would you do that?"

"I would have a way, or I would find a way."

"You don't make enough money to pay for all the loans and run a house." Mark shook his head. "Karen needs a husband with means to lift her and us out of this, and that is not you."

"And you'll never have a car like this."

Mark chuckled. "You're right at that." He sighed. "But I do not need a car like this. We Amish drive buggies."

"Well, isn't that what *Rumspringa* is for? You could go off on *Rumspringa* and buy a car and have all kinds of fun racing around with it. You could work in the *Englisch* world, make *gut* money to buy one of these." He slapped his hand on the hood of the car. "Would you get a red one, too, Mark?"

"Dark blue, almost black." Mark clutched the receipt book to his side. "Is that what you did, Nicodemus? Did you go on a wild *Rumspringa*? Did you break all the rules and have fast cars and women beside you?"

"Not so wild, but *jah*, I went to New York with some of my friends. We had fun, but—"

"But you came back to our way of life? This wonderful life where you rent a room on a farm far out in the country and have your meals cooked by a young woman? Hmm, kind of a sad story, do not you think?" Mark was suddenly baiting him, for he always felt there was more to Nicodemus than met the eye. There was a story somewhere with this boarder, and he wished the man would just tell it. "I have to take this inside right now, but maybe later you will tell me the story about your *Rumspringa*. I would like to hear it."

"Maybe. Later then." It seemed that Nicodemus recoiled, folding in on himself a bit.

Karen had made enough small talk with the banker. "Where did you go to get the receipt book, Mark, clear to Chicago?"

"I am sorry. I was delayed talking to Nicodemus."

She scowled, "We have been waiting. Go ahead, Mr. London, please write the receipt." She eased herself up on her arms to sit more upright, but grimaced when she pushed accidentally with her injured arm.

"I am sorry you were hurt so badly." Mr. London handed her the hurriedly written receipt. "It was an accident, was it not?"

"A buggy accident near the bridge. My youngest brother was in the hospital at the time. On the way back home, the buggy wheel must have loosened, as far as we can tell, plunging us near the river. I broke my leg and arm and of course, and you can see my face is still cut and bruised. They tell me I nearly died of hyperthermia. Thankfully, I do not have much recollection."

Jace London nodded. "I'm so sorry, Karen. What a horrible ordeal. How could you even survive such a thing?"

"*Gott* had a hand in my survival, Mr. London. Do you believe in *Gott*?"

"Well, as much as most folks. I believe in something bigger than me." He ran his finger around his collar, seemingly in discomfort.

She smiled. "That is *gut*. In difficult times, we need to hold fast to our faith."

He shook his head. "I feel badly about your circumstances. I mean, you have not even recovered."

"Thank you," she said, realizing that perhaps there was a compassionate side to him, after all.

He stood. "Let me make a call. Excuse me for a moment."

He walked outside to the porch, and she heard him talking, but she could not make out his words. Within a few moments, he was back.

"I am able to refund you half. Just for this month as you have been hit by so much, your brother and now you. So many hospital expenses ahead of you. The bank wants to ease the burden at least temporarily."

She gaped at him. "Th-Thank you," she stammered. "And you're right. Our hospital bills will be large." She didn't want to tell him they had no insurance. Amish folks didn't believe in insurance. They took care of their own like *Gott* told them to do. She would have to appeal to the district to use the emergency fund, but she was determined to eventually pay that emergency fund back.

He gave her a sad smile. "Will you have to sell the farm?"

Karen took a deep breath. "Perhaps, Mr. London. There may be no other way out of our debts. My brother, John, is leaving to work in Indiana and my other two brothers and I could move to a cottage or apartment if I end up having to sell the farm." She gave a rueful smile. "That should make the bank happy, as I would then be able to pay the entire debt back."

He cleared his throat. "Well, I personally wouldn't be happy to see you sell the farm. I am aware of how much it means to you. I also know your parents worked very hard to acquire this farm, and they wanted to keep it."

"I promised my *mamm*..." Karen started and then stopped abruptly. Why in the world would she share such things with this man? She must be losing her mind.

He waited for her to continue, but when she didn't, he said, "Again, it gives the bank no pleasure to see folks lose their homes."

Karen sighed. "It might be time to let it go."

He only looked at her. Karen ran her hand along the top of the sofa. *Why would he not leave? She had her receipt. He had his money.*

At that moment, Felix entered the living room. "What is going on here?" He gazed at the banker. "And you are—"

"Jace London. With the bank. I was just leaving." Before he turned to go, Jace added, "Let me know what you decide, Karen." And then he left, leaving the scent of his men's cologne to linger in the air.

Mark and Stuart followed him out—perhaps to ensure that he left.

Felix sat down on the edge of the sofa. He sat there quietly watching her for some time, seeming to gather his wits to speak. "Karen, I know that I keep asking, but I am asking again. Marry me. I know that I am not a hero on a white stead, like the *Englisch* fairy tales. I am not much on the eyes, but I am a *gut* Amish man of strong faith. When you marry me, John would no longer be obliged to leave for Indiana to make money for the farm. You would not have to sell the farm your parents worked so hard and long to acquire. You could keep your promise to your *mamm*—to care for your brothers and the farm. You will never toil over money like this again. You know that I love you, and in time, I believe you will come to love me. Marry me."

A sharp pain shot through Karen's leg again, bringing tears to her eyes, or maybe, the tears were already there ready to flow down her cheeks. He had reached for her hand, but then, he withdrew it, perhaps fearing he would be rejected yet again. His words echoed through the room.

Karen shifted. "I-I will think on it tonight, and tell you my decision in the morning."

Felix sighed. "*Jah*, in the morning then." His voice was tired. "Shall I get Mark to help you to bed?"

She silently nodded. She saw his kind brown eyes were glossy, and she feared he might cry, too. But he ran his hand slowly over his chin; stood up and took off his hat. She saw his balding head. He bit on his lower lip for a moment. "Shall I make you a cup of hot tea for Stuart to bring to you once you are settled back in your room?"

"That would be nice, Felix. *Danke*."

Chapter Seven

That evening Karen wrote in her journal.

Dear Journal,

I do not know what to do. I don't want to say gut-bye to my dear sweet brother, John. How can he be sent to Indiana away from his family just to save this forsaken farm? Jah, we have been through much lately. I see the pain in Mark's and Stuart's faces. Boys to men in such a short time. Yet, I have the answer to all of their woes.

A sharp invasive knock at her bedroom door stopped her pen. "*Jah?*"

"It's Kevin Olson. May I have a word?"

"*Jah*, come in Mr. Olson. But please leave the door open." Under normal circumstances, she would never allow a boarder to come to her room. But these weren't normal circumstances, and her room had become more of a sitting room than a bedroom.

Kevin opened the door and stepped only one foot inside the room. He cleared his throat. "I have come to give notice. I've found a new apartment in town. I am finding it difficult with no television and no electricity. So, I will be moving out before the next month's rent is due. Really, I don't know how you people live like this your whole lives. I am near going crazy with no stimulation whatsoever."

She smiled at him, not surprised. "I did tell you the Amish life is not an easy life for an *Englischer*. *Jah*, I think you will be happier in town, Kevin. Besides, there are likely to be some changes around here anyway."

"How are you feeling? I felt terrible that you had such a bad accident. I'm glad it wasn't worse."

"*Danke*, Mr. Olson." She smiled. "I do wish you well, and I know you have made the best decision."

"I thought you would be upset because you need money, and now I am leaving you with a deficit."

Karen took a deep breath and straightened her shoulders. "*Gott* will provide, Mr. Olson. He always does."

"That's another thing, this blind faith. I don't get it. All this work and work and no joy."

She frowned. "But we do have joy. We have our families, our friends, and our work. I know that our ways are sometimes difficult to understand."

"Well, if it means anything, I believe I am a better person for having lived here. I learned a lot about Amish life, maybe about life in general. Enough to know that I can't hack it here." He laughed.

She laughed with him.

He stood silent for a moment, then said, "I'll be packing up my things then and leaving. Thank you for everything, Miss Helmuth."

"You are welcome. *Gut* luck. *Gott segen eich*."

"Uh, thanks. Thanks a lot."

As he left her room, she thought, *Maybe Gott has chosen you for something special, Kevin, and you just do not know it yet.*

She returned to her journal:

Kevin Olson gave his notice. He is leaving. We shall be short the money from his room.

She paused to close her eyes. *Mamm what were you thinking? Why did you leave me with this?*

Chapter Eight

Felix wore his best pants and shirt for the wedding. He brushed his hat until it appeared new, or nearly new. He was freshly shaved and had combed what hair he had so that it did not stick out every which way. He knew there was absolutely nothing he could do about his stomach, which protruded over the top of his pants, but he refused to indulge in regret. The belly was what it was for a man of forty-nine.

Karen wore her Sunday blue dress and a freshly laundered apron. Her new white *kapp* glistened on the bureau. Today she would become Felix Sutter's wife. She would no longer have to worry about her brothers. John would no longer have to go to Indiana. The farm debt would be paid. She would go to live in Felix's house, and her brothers could live in their own debt-free home.

Of course, they were welcome to stay at Felix's house whenever they wished, and they would likely take many of their meals over there.

Nicodemus was beside himself. When he first heard that Karen had decided to marry the old man Sutter, he paced back and forth in the kitchen. It could not be so. He should have told her how much he loved her. There was still time. He could still tell her. He would profess his love today while there was still time. She was not married yet. She had not spoken her vows-yet.

But...when he saw her, it seemed *Gott* had tied his tongue. He did not speak to her. She was dressed in her best blue dress. She had on the white *kapp*. She was ready to marry Felix Sutter.

His eyes locked the briefest of moments with hers, and the lump in his throat became so huge that there was no way he could tell her. She had tears in her eyes. Were they tears of sadness? Were they tears of joy? He wanted to comfort her, to console her, to tell her that all would be fine, and that she did not have to marry Felix—he could take care of her just as well as the old man. But he knew his words would not speak the truth. Nicodemus knew in his heart, that no matter how much he loved her, he could never take care of her, the brothers, and the farm. He could do nothing for her. *Nothing.* He could only love her and that was not enough. If he loved her, and he did with all his heart, he would let her be.

That was exactly what he did. He hurried out of the kitchen, like a rat suddenly exposed to the daylight.

Nicodemus did not attend the wedding. He passed the time behind the barn whittling, waiting until the ceremony was over. Then, he would come out of his hiding. He would congratulate Felix Sutter on his marriage to Karen Helmuth. He would wish them both happiness. He would. But he could not do so now. Now, Nicodemus Imhoff sulked in the shadows, waiting for it all to end, waiting for Felix to take his new wife to his home, out of Nicodemus' sight.

Chapter Nine

Dear Journal,

Well, I am married. I know that my husband is a gut *man. I know he loves me, but why can I not love him? Why do I torment myself with thoughts of Nicodemus? Felix is so kind to me and patient. He makes me laugh so many times during the day, but I cannot get Nicodemus out of my mind...*

"How is your leg today, *liebling?*"

"I think it is repairing as it does not bother me as much lately."

Felix smiled, "*Gut, gut.* Here is some nice hot tea. Winter is coming, I am afraid." He placed a quilt over her on the sofa. "May I get you a cookie to go with your tea?"

"*Denki,* Felix, you are much too *gut* to me." It was true. He was much too good. "I am ready to begin my own chores in the house. I am your *frau,* and I know it would be nice for me to have a nice hot meal when you come in from your work. Were you with my brothers today?"

"*Jah.* Those boys are hard workers. Even young Stuart is proving to be a fine young man and hard worker. You did well by your upbringing of your brothers, Karen."

As she sipped her tea, she watched him sit down in his rocker with his Bible on his knees. He reminded her so much of her father and how he would sit by the fire, his glasses slipping down on his nose while he read.

He clearly felt her eyes on him. "Do you need anything?"

"I was wondering, uh, is Nicodemus helping on the farm, too?"

"*Jah,* when he is not at work, he helps your brothers. He talks of owning his own farm soon with his savings. For a man who began with a lazy outlook, he has stepped up."

She adjusted the quilt around her. "He did not like his job at the lumberyard and always said he would save for a business or a farm of his own."

Felix pushed his glasses up higher onto the bridge of his nose, "Apparently, he is almost there, for a down payment, anyway. He did go looking for farms, I believe, so soon we shall lose his rent money, but it is just as well. The boys will be thinking of courting soon, especially John. I think he may even be courting now, though he has not confided in me."

She sat up, tipping her teacup, spilling a few drops on the quilt. "Oh *nee*. I have made a mess on the quilt."

"I will fetch you another quilt." He went off to the cupboard, whistling his favorite tune. When he returned, his hand brushed hers, and he grasped it lightly. "I do love you so much, dear, Karen."

He waited for her response, but Karen had never told him she loved him. Never. She was courteous, even kind. But she could not say the words. He was unable to suppress his sigh. "Eh, knock, knock." He was starting one of his silly little jokes that always made her giggle.

"Who is there?" she asked automatically. After weeks of his antics, she knew what her response should be.

"Weekend."

"Weekend who?"

"We are married, and weekend do anything we want."

Neither of them laughed. She put on a smile, but the air between them was strained. What he wanted most, she had not given him.

"I have to go check on the cows, and I will be back as soon as I can." He tucked the clean quilt around her.

Soon as he left the house, Karen grabbed her cane, but then, she tossed it across the room in frustration. She walked without it to the bedroom. She took her journal out of the drawer and began to write. The journal was her only outlet now. There was no one to listen to her, no one to share her thoughts with, only writing.

Dear Journal,

Oh, the mess I have found myself in. I have sacrificed my own happiness so that my brothers can have their home and the farm. No one paused a moment to ask, what would make Karen happy? Not one person. John will likely be marrying a girl he loves. He is going to have happiness. Here I am, married to a man who is a kind husband, but I do not love him. I have tried. Gott *knows that I have tried. But I cannot stop thinking about Nicodemus. If only I could have had held on a little longer and not married Felix.*

I would be with Nicodemus on his farm when he gets one, and we could have our family and live forever happily, but now, now I am stuck here in a loveless, unhappy life. But how could I have waited? That Jace London was going to get the farm. My brothers had suffered so much and were working so hard. I was the only one with a solution.

I am so torn and so miserable. Oh journal, all of this because I made an unfair promise to my mamm. *How could she ask her* dochter *for such a promise?*

Karen put her hand to her aching head. She felt so tired. She dressed for bed, climbed between the cold sheets, and closed her eyes. She could only escape in her dreams now. She could only hope that in her dreams Nicodemus would hold her; that he would whisper into her ear and tell her everything would be all right.

Felix was surprised to find his wife already asleep when he returned. He tried to be as quiet as possible when he climbed into bed. Then he lifted himself up on one elbow so that he could stare at her sleeping face in the shadows. He saw beads of sweat on her forehead. He placed his hand gently on her forehead and felt the burning heat. *Karen was ill.* She was burning up with fever. He immediately got up and went to the kitchen for tepid water to rub her down to cool her off.

"What is this? What are you doing? *Mamm? Mamm?*" She was delirious with fever.

"Karen, you are ill, we have to bring down your fever." He made her take sips of water. He changed out the cloth on her head to keep her cool. She thrashed in the bed, entangling the blankets around her. The sheets became soaked with her sweat.

For three days and nights, Felix did not leave her side. Even when the local herbal woman, Mrs. Bruker, came at his request, he refused to leave the room. She offered to stay until Karen improved, but still, Felix would not budge from her bedside. Karen's brothers came by and helped with outside chores every morning, for which Felix was completely grateful. He wouldn't leave Karen to do them.

Finally, by the sixth morning, she lay quietly sleeping.

Felix was beyond exhausted. He could hardly see straight from lack of sleep and worry. He slogged his way to the kitchen to make her a fresh pot of tea. He warmed a biscuit and smoothed marmalade on it, taking it back to her.

"Here my dearest, a bit of tea and a biscuit. You have not eaten in days." He placed the tray on the nightstand. "Let me help with your pillow so you can sit up." He gave her a weary smile of total relief. "Feeling better?"

"*Jah*, I-I've been very sick, haven't I? I must have caught a bug."

"A nasty one that fought with you for six days and nights, but you look much improved, my dearest." He leaned in to kiss her forehead, and he felt her stiffen. "Eat your biscuit now. I will check on the cows and be right back."

John had already been by that morning to see to the livestock, but now, Felix needed an excuse to leave her side for a moment. He walked slowly out of the bedroom; he was so exhausted. Would Karen ever take down the walls she had put up around her? Would she *ever* come to love him?

Outside, in the barn, he patted his milk cow's nose. "How are you doing, ol' girl?" Brownie mooed loudly. "Okay, okay. Seems all the women around me are sensitive nowadays."

He sighed and closed his eyes.

Chapter Ten

Days went by and then weeks. John announced his upcoming marriage to a young girl named Sarah. They were deeply in love which everyone could see.

Karen did not care for her.

Felix implored her, "Karen, I don't understand your resistance to your brother's intended. Sarah is *gut* for him, and he is happy. I have never seen him so happy since your parents' deaths. She is shoulder to shoulder with him working on the farm. She is out in the fields at his side."

"I fear she may just be after the farm, that is the point. She helps him now, but we will see how long it continues once they are married."

"My sweet, she loves him. That is quite evident. They will have a loving life together."

Karen shook her head, "A marriage needs strength. A marriage needs commitment to the commitment. It does not need all this sweetness."

Felix smiled sadly. "That sweetness, as you call it, is love."

"Love?" she asked, swiping her hand across her forehead. "Marriage is not only about love. It is about shouldering responsibility and being practical. Marriage is not a fairytale. You know that, Felix." Her words were harsh. "I only want John to know that, too, and this girl, Sarah, does she know it? Marriage is work."

Felix's smile left his lips. He slowly walked out of the room—his heart heavy. He now knew Karen would never love him like he loved her. His love would have to be enough.

As soon as Felix left the house, Karen began to write in her journal again.

Dear Journal,

I cannot bear all this talk of love one moment longer while the man I love is planning to leave my childhood farm and buy his own home without me in it. How can I keep going while everyone else has true love and happy lives? I thought it would be enough that Felix paid off our debts and that the farm was safe, but it is not enough, it truly is not. I think of Nicodemus night and day. What would our lives have been if I had married him? Oh, if only...

But life went on, as it always did. Cows were milked. Chicks were hatched. Calves were born.

"Felix, I am going out to the coop. I want to see how many chicks have hatched."

"*Jah*, there are quite a few. We can keep them all if you like." He smiled. It was good to see Karen up and about, showing an active interest in things. She moved freely these days, too, without her cane.

"I'll be a while," she said. "I want to think about next year's garden, too. I enjoy thinking about planting and harvesting the vegetables. And I know you have seed catalogs in the barn."

"Take your time," he said, maintaining his smile.

He watched her leave. He thought he could be strong forever; he thought he could be patient forever, but he was beginning to doubt himself—and that was a constant worry. He went into the kitchen and put a kettle on for tea.

"Dearest *Gott*, she makes me weak in my stomach." He cast his eyes toward heaven. "I thought I could bear it, but I cannot not. I thought she would come to love me, but she has not. *Gott*, she does her wifely duties, but her heart is never in any of those duties. There is no love."

He went to his rocker and collapsed into the seat. His mind went to a familiar Bible verse about husbands loving their wives. He'd loved Karen for years. Years and years, it seemed, and what good had it done?

He blew out his breath and closed his eyes for a moment. Was there anything else he could possibly do? Anything?

He opened his eyes and looked about the room. It was fairly tidy, but there were things he could do. It was unusual for a man to do a woman's cleaning tasks, but he'd never been usual. Perhaps he could touch Karen's heart if he helped with some of her chores.

He went into the washroom for cloths and a broom. He went through the house and tidied everything he saw that needed it. He felt like a bachelor again, and his spirit cringed at the feeling.

He went into their bedroom. He straightened the quilts on the bed, smoothing them down. He dusted the bureau top and the side tables. He went to close the drawer on Karen's side of the bed, and he saw her journal through the small crack of the open drawer. He slowly slid open the drawer. He stared at the book with the word 'Journal' written on the front. He ran his finger over the word several times before he gently lifted the book out. He sat on the bed, fingering the binding. He had never kept a journal, but he knew that some women seemed to enjoy doing so.

He knew he should not open it. He knew he should not read it. These were Karen's private thoughts, yet the more he told himself he had no right to her private thoughts, the more he wanted to know what those thoughts were.

He chided himself. "Do not read her journal. Do not read it."

But he did.

And the words immediately jumped off the pages and ripped his heart in half. On the last page he read the words, "... *I think of Nicodemus night and day...*" over and over again.

He closed the journal and slipped the book back into the drawer. He properly closed the drawer all the way, leaving no crack.

Then, he sealed off his heart...

Chapter Eleven

Karen came rushing into the kitchen. "Felix. There are three dozen new chicks. Unheard of. Three *dozen*. Can you imagine?" She saw that the kitchen was sparkling clean. Everything was stored neatly on the shelves. She stopped short. "Oh my."

But Felix was not in the kitchen. As she walked through the rooms of the house, it was apparent that Felix had gone out of his way to tidy up. "Felix? Are you here?"

"I am in the front room, Karen."

She rushed into the front room. "*Denki,* Felix. Everything looks so nice. You should not have done that for me, but *denki*." She was genuinely happy. "There are three dozen new chicks. Can you imagine? Three *dozen*."

He was sitting quietly in his rocker with his Bible on his knees. He answered quietly as he removed his glasses and put them on the small table next to him. "Three dozen. *Nee*, I cannot imagine that many chicks." His voice was flat. His straw hat was on the table next to his chair, so his balding head was exposed, making him appear even older than he was.

"Is everything all right?" she asked, feeling genuine concern. His face was blanched white.

"*Nee*, Karen. Everything is not all right. Nothing is all right. I have done a wrong, and the truth of the matter is, now I must pay the price. I am stunned, but I deserve such a shock for my indifference to your plight. I ... I read your journal, Karen."

He intently watched her face. He saw her shock and then anger and then resignation.

His throat hurt, but he managed to say, "Please gather your things, pack them up, and move back to your farm with your brothers. I am sure you will be much happier there on your own farm, given the uh, well, the *situation*. I will think of something to tell the folks in the community. Maybe that your brothers have need of you. But do not return here again, Karen. You are no longer ... needed."

She didn't move. She didn't even breathe. "Felix, I—" And then she took a gasping breath. "I... You... How could you have read it?"

He nodded, his face sad beyond description. "It was unforgivable and a true breach of marital trust. But what does it matter now?" He put the Bible on the side table, stood up and said, "I will get the buggy to load up your things. Do you need help gathering them?"

She whispered, "*Nee*. I-I ... don't have much here. Mostly my clothes." It was true. She had left all her belongings back at her family farmhouse since Felix had a well-equipped home. She had not even had to bring linens or towels or quilts.

He nodded and left her standing there.

At first, she was too stunned to move. And then her eyes burned with tears. What had she done? *What had she done?*

That look on Felix's face. The hurt. The crush of betrayal. She began to weep. She was a *horrible* person. Horrible and cruel. What was the matter with her?

Ach, what had she done?

How could she go back to her brothers? What would she say? Maybe her brothers would not even want her to return. John was undoubtedly going to bring his new wife into the home and then, of course, there was the matter of Nicodemus.

With halting steps, she stumbled to the bedroom to pack her clothes.

Chapter Twelve

Karen's brothers were delighted to have her stay with them. They thought it was only for a short while because of whatever Felix had told them. She wasn't sure what he'd said.

Stuart kept saying, "Finally, you are back. I told them you would not abandon us to John's food forever." And then he laughed.

"*Nee*, I ... knew you needed me," she said. But it wasn't true. Granted, right after she was married, it might have been true, but over the months her brothers had worked things out and the house ran smoothly now.

Mark shook his head. "But you are married as we all know. We won't get too used to you again. This won't be permanent."

"Right," Karen said with a forced laugh.

Mark smiled. "I have to admit, I am with Stuart on this one. I sure have missed your cooking. Not that I'm not happy to see you, too, but oh, to have *gut* food again."

She began to laugh, but Nicodemus came into the kitchen. She wondered what he had overheard. She stopped laughing. "Nicodemus."

"Karen, are you here for a while? I've missed you—, uh, and your cooking, too, of course." He pulled out a kitchen chair and sat down as if he was shocked.

"Thank you," she said, hearing the slight tremor in her voice.

"I try to keep an eye on your brothers, especially with John so preoccupied with his Sarah." He grinned, now clearly relaxing. "Well, I am very glad that you have returned for a while. Very glad indeed."

Mark sat in the kitchen chair between them. "Nico, remember, Karen is a married woman now. She is off limits." He was teasing, but there was an edge in his voice.

"*Ach*," Nicodemus responded, "Don't fret. I have my own girlfriend now."

The room became suddenly quiet.

"Do you?" Karen found her voice.

Nicodemus smiled widely. "Her name is Anne. She lives in the next district over. I mean, well, she does not know my feelings yet, but I want to court her. You would like her, Karen, she is a lot like you. Self-sufficient, a farm girl."

Karen swallowed. "How ... nice for you."

"Now I can afford to put down a payment on a farm. I have been looking at a few, and I will have something to offer her." He smiled again, clearly pleased.

Mark slapped his friend's back. "That is great news, Nico. We're so happy for you. Well, it seems all the men are going to be gone soon, and it will be just Stuart and me left to fend for ourselves."

Karen got up to put a kettle on the stove. She kept her back to them. "Well, I am still here with you for now. Tea?" she asked.

In unison they answered, "*Jah*."

She felt like she might scream, but she moved about the kitchen, fetching teacups, getting biscuits and marmalade out. Her eyes burned with tears, but she held them back. How would it be to cry in front of Nicodemus and her brothers now? They would see her as the total fool she was, that was for sure and for certain.

Nicodemus was in love. Her bottom lip quivered. She felt ridiculous, like a thwarted teenager on *Rumspringa*. She poured the tea into two cups and placed one in front of Mark and the other in front of Nicodemus.

Mark asked, "Aren't you having tea with us?"

"*Nee*, I see this house needs a *gut* cleaning. Felix was right to send me over here. There is laundry stacked to the moon, and these floors need a *gut* sweep. Drink your tea. I am going to get started on cleaning. It may take me weeks to get this place put to rights again." Of course, she was exaggerating, but she needed something to focus on something besides her own stupidity and disappointment.

Mark grinned. "Looks like we are going to have weeks of *gut* suppers again." He nudged Nicodemus' side.

The weeks dragged on. Karen adjusted to the idea of Nicodemus with another girl. In truth, it wasn't as heartbreaking as she'd feared. Somehow, she had made the idea of Nicodemus huge in her mind—but the reality wasn't quite the same. She cared for him, of course, but the blinding passion she had imagined was not there.

Oddly, she found herself thinking about Felix more and more. She missed his whistling in the morning as he put the kettle on for tea before she even got out of bed. And there was no one to gently put a coverlet over her in the evenings when she read her Bible. She had tried a knock-knock joke on Stuart, but his response was, "That is as dumb as a doornail. Do people laugh at those things?"

One afternoon, she found herself alone with Nicodemus at the table. John and her brothers had gone to town to pick up supplies. She put a bowl of hot soup in front of him and one for herself at the other end of the table.

"Ah, Karen, bring that bowl down here. It is just the two of us and why should we have to shout." He chuckled warmly.

She carried her soup bowl to his end of the table. He bowed his head to say the silent blessing. She had dreamt of this moment, sitting at the kitchen table with Nicodemus, eating together. She was aware of his nearness as he began to pray, but when he cleared his throat and the prayer was over, she realized she didn't feel much of anything. There were no romantic stirrings in her heart. She watched him slurp his chicken soup. Had he always eaten so noisily?

"*Gut* soup. You will have to teach my Anne how to make it once we are married." He chuckled. "Wait. What do I know? Maybe she already makes delicious soup."

Karen looked at him. Nicodemus had moved on in his life. *Had she?* She continued to watch him devour the soup. She thought about how Felix ate her soup, slowly and quietly.

Later in the day, she took the family buggy to Felix's farm. She couldn't help it. She wanted to be there, to see if everything was all right. She'd already gone a few times before when she knew he wouldn't be there. The first time she had gone, she'd walked from room to room to see if he had changed anything, but he had not.

That day, she had slowly opened the drawer next to her side of the bed and saw that her journal was still sitting in there, like a guilty testament, daring her to open the pages and read her own horrible words. When she had left so hurriedly those weeks before, she hadn't wanted to even touch it, she'd felt so guilty for what she'd written.

But that day, she took it from the drawer and carried it unceremoniously into the living room. She built a fire and threw the journal on top of the red and yellow flames. She did not watch it burn, but instead, hurried back into the kitchen where she tidied the shelves. She put a soup on the stove for Felix to eat when he returned.

One afternoon when she had gone over there, she had toiled over making bread, and Felix returned earlier than expected. He had not spoken to her. He'd gone into the bathroom and cleaned up and changed. He'd carried his soiled clothes to the washroom, placing the mud-stained clothing into the laundry basket. He sat down at the table and let her serve him the roasted chicken she had made to go along with the hot bread. She did not speak, either. Nor did she sit with him at the table. She busied herself cleaning up the kitchen. Then, she left.

The next time she had come to cook, she put on her best blue dress, her bright white apron and white *kapp*. She had planned on making him a nice roast with potatoes and carrots. She noticed his work horse was in the corral, along with the buggy horse. Still, she hoped he wasn't there. She could work much more freely if he weren't at home. When she entered the kitchen, it was unusually cold. No fire had been made in the fireplace. Quickly, she started one. She began to assemble the ingredients for the roast dinner and placed them on the counter. And then, she heard a deep moan coming from the bedroom.

She peeked in the door and saw him fully clothed lying on top of the bed. She ran to his side and put her hand on his forehead. He was warm, and his face was pale. "*Ach*, Felix... Come on, let us get you under the covers." He didn't respond. His eyes were closed, and he kept moaning, as if in pain.

When he opened his eyes, he looked disoriented. "Karen, Karen? Where are you, Karen?"

"Oh, poor dear, dear sweet Felix. I'll help you now." Her heart hurt just looking at how miserable he was. "I'm here," she said. She made him more comfortable, though she wasn't sure he was even aware of it. He did not open his eyes again. "I'm going to go for the Mrs. Bruker. She will have something to give you that will help."

She put a cool, wet cloth on his head, but he threw it off. She placed it again, more firmly.

"I am going now. I will be right back as soon as I can. It will be all right." She hurried out of the room. She was reluctant to leave him, but there was no other way. She had to get something to help him feel better.

Mrs. Bruker came quickly. She had a bag full of small bottles and herbs. "How long has he been like this?" She felt Felix's forehead.

"I-I do not know. When I got here to cook, he was like this. The house was cold, no coals in the fireplace. Maybe two days since I came last."

Mrs. Bruker locked eyes with Karen. "You are not living with your husband?"

"We, uh, well, I have been staying with my brothers for a while. The eldest is getting married and the two younger ones..."

The herb lady put her hands on her hips and stared at her. "Bring your brothers here if you must. But you do not leave your husband unattended for your siblings. Your duty is to your husband." Mrs. Bruker huffed a sigh and went into the kitchen to prepare her herbs.

Karen sat on the edge of the bed, feeling properly chastised. She knew Mrs. Bruker was right, and she was ashamed of herself. Her shame and regret had been growing for many days, and now she couldn't ignore her feelings a moment longer.

"I am so sorry, Felix," she whispered, leaning close to his ear. "I have not been a *gut* wife. I realize it now. I was so very, very wrong." She knew he could not hear her in his condition, but she vowed to herself, as soon as he was well... Then, the horror struck her. *What if Felix never got well? What if he died before he knew...before he knew that she did care for him after all.*

She had never said it. She had never thought it, but now, being near him like this, she knew. She knew she loved him.

Mrs. Bruker returned and felt his pulse. She shook her head. "He may need the hospital. It's as if he has given up his will." She looked into Karen's face. "What is truly going on here?"

Karen was silent, but she stroked Felix's shoulder. "I want to help," she said softly.

Mrs. Bruker shook her head. "Fine. I will explain what to do with these herbs. The rest is up to *Gott* and Felix himself."

"B-But he has to live," Karen cried. "I-I have to tell him I'm sorry. He *has* to live." She began to cry softly.

The herb woman shrugged her shoulders, but her expression was one of compassion. "We always think we have more time to say or do the things we know we should. But what did Jesus tell us? *We know not the hour*...and sometimes there is no more time..."

The woman placed her hand on Karen's shaking shoulders. "There, there. Things just might turn around now. Shall I stay with you?"

Karen shook her head. "I-I'm all right. *Denki* for coming to help. How can I pay you?"

"Chickens and maybe a loaf of bread or two." The herbal woman smiled. "I hope there is much more time for you two."

Karen sat next to the bed in the darkness, holding Felix's hand. She hummed softly into the stagnant air.

Felix opened his eyes. He looked confused and then frowned. "Wh-What are you doing here?" He pulled his hand away from Karen's.

"I have been taking care of you, Felix. You've been very ill."

"I-I don't need you here. I'm better now."

Karen took a deep breath. Her hand was shaking; her entire body was shaking. She prayed Felix would be open to her. She prayed she hadn't destroyed all the love he used to feel for her.

"Felix, don't make me leave. Please. I-I love you. I am still your wife. I can't leave. And maybe you still love me. You called my name over and over when you were sick."

"The rantings of a fool," he mumbled, turned away from her.

"I've been here for two days. I haven't left," she said, her voice pleading, hoping he'd give her another chance. "I've been a fool for ... months and months. I-I love you."

And there they were again. The three words he had waited for and hoped to hear for so long. He tried to sit up, but he was too weak. Karen helped him.

"Felix, I was so wrong. I was ... foolish from the very beginning. You are a wonderful husband, a *gut* man. I am blessed."

She kissed his forehead, praying he wouldn't push her away. "Can you forgive me?"

His brown eyes filled with tears. He was silent for a long moment—so long she feared he wouldn't respond at all.

And then finally, he said, "Do you mean it?"

She looked at him with total sincerity. "I mean it."

He took a heaving gulp of breath. His eyes filled with tears. "Then, there is nothing to forgive, *liebling*. Your love just needed time to catch up to the depth of my love for you." He pulled himself up even further to a sitting position.

She leaned over him, weeping, and kissed his forehead, his cheeks, his lips.

"Felix?"

He grabbed both her hands. "*Jah?*"

"Thank you." She could hardly contain her gratitude.

He smiled at her through his tears and shook his head. He cleared his throat and gave her such a look of love that she trembled all over. "*Nee, liebling*," he said, his voice thick with emotion. "It is I who thank you."

The End

Continue Reading...

Thank you for reading **_Keeping the Family Together._** Are you wondering **what to read next?** Why not read **_An Amish Café?_ Here's a peek for you:**

Dorothy sat quietly in the fields as the dry wind danced past, causing the grass at her feet to tickle her skin. The birds chirped around her, and the warm setting sun cast a golden glow on her peaceful surroundings. She fixed her gaze on the horizon with endless rows of crops swaying ever-so-slightly in the playful breeze and wondered if anything about her life would ever change.

Dorothy knew what she had to do and what her community expected: find a husband, settle down, and start having children. The only problem was that whenever she saw all her friends doing this, her stomach turned uncomfortably, and her palms began sweating.

"Dorothy... Dorothy!"

Dorothy's head shot up at the sound of her name, pulling her out of her sad, anxious thoughts. She turned to see her mother standing outside the barn door, squinting against the setting sun, looking for her.

Dorothy murmured, "Coming, *Mamm*," as she rose to her feet, wiping her sweaty palms while brushing the dirt from her skirts. She approached the house and her waiting mother.

"There you are," Bernice said as she saw her daughter walking toward her.

Dorothy gave her mother a fond smile. "I'm here. What do you need?"

Bernice studied Dorothy curiously for a moment before she nodded. "It's about time we started on dinner." She turned and walked back into the house.

Dorothy frowned briefly at her mother's strange behavior before she shrugged and followed Bernice into the kitchen.

"So, what's the plan for dinner?" Dorothy inquired as she scrubbed her hands at the kitchen sink. The water from the cold tap was lukewarm after spending a long, warm day in the pipes.

"Nothing fancy, just some casserole. I don't have much energy for anything more than that."

"That's fine, *Mamm*; it shouldn't take long." Dorothy wiped her hands on a nearby dishtowel and walked over to the kitchen counter. She then took a knife from the drawer and an onion from the vegetable rack before rolling up her sleeves and getting to work. "I can even make it myself if you'd like to rest."

Bernice shook her head as she began gathering the remaining ingredients. "No need, *liebchen*, I enjoy cooking."

VISIT HERE To Read More!

https://www.ticahousepublishing.com/amish-miller.html

Thank you for Reading

If you **love Amish Romance**, **Visit Here:**

https://amish.subscribemenow.com/

to find out about all **New Hannah Miller Amish Romance Releases!** **We will let you know as soon as they become available!**

If you enjoyed *Keeping the Family Together,* would you kindly take a couple minutes to leave a positive review on Amazon? It only takes a moment, and positive reviews truly make a difference. I would be so grateful! Thank you!

Turn the page to discover more Hannah Miller Amish Romances just for you!

More Amish Romance from Hannah Miller

Visit HERE for Hannah Miller's Amish Romance

https://ticahousepublishing.com/amish-miller.html

About the Author

Hannah Miller has been writing Amish Romance for the past seven years. Long intrigued by the Amish way of life, Hannah has traveled the United States, visiting different Amish communities. She treasures her Amish friends and enjoys visiting with them. Hannah makes her home in Indiana, along with her husband, Robert. Together, they have three children and seven grandchildren. Hannah loves to ride bikes in the sunshine. And if it's warm enough for a picnic, you'll find her under the nearest tree!

Made in United States
North Haven, CT
30 July 2023

39732569R00065